Tsunamis

Andrea Rivera

abdopublishing.com

Published by Abdo Zoom™, PO Box 398166, Minneapolis, Minnesota 55439. Copyright © 2018 by Abdo Consulting Group, Inc. International copyrights reserved in all countries. No part of this book may be reproduced in any form without written permission from the publisher. Abdo Zoom™ is a trademark and logo of Abdo Consulting Group, Inc.

Printed in the United States of America, North Mankato, Minnesota
042017
092017

Cover Photo: Jiji Press/AFP/Getty Images
Interior Photos: Jiji Press/AFP/Getty Images, 1; Kyodo News/AP Images, 4–5; iStockphoto, 6–7; Franck Robichon/EPA/Newscom, 8; Bob Bush Photo/iStockphoto, 9; NOAA, 11; Lars Nicolaysen/picture-alliance/dpa/AP Images, 13; Chayatorn Laorattanavech/Shutterstock Images, 14; Shutterstock Images, 15; John Orsbun/Shutterstock Images, 16–17; Jeff Barnard/AP Images, 17; Paulo Oliveira/Shutterstock Images, 19; Christian Vinces/Shutterstock Images, 21

Editor: Brienna Rossiter
Series Designer: Madeline Berger
Art Direction: Dorothy Toth

Publisher's Cataloging-in-Publication Data
Names: Rivera, Andrea, author.
Title: Tsunamis / by Andrea Rivera.
Description: Minneapolis, MN : Abdo Zoom, 2018. | Series: Natural disasters | Includes bibliographical references and index.
Identifiers: LCCN 2017930337 | ISBN 9781532120404 (lib. bdg.) | ISBN 9781614797517 (ebook) | ISBN 9781614798071 (Read-to-me ebook)
Subjects: LCSH: Tsunamis--Juvenile literature.
Classification: DDC 363.34/94--dc23
LC record available at http://lccn.loc.gov/2017930337

Table of Contents

Tsunamis are huge waves.
The waves begin deep underwater.

4

An **earthquake** shakes the ocean floor. This pushes up lots of water.

5

The waves start small. As they move toward shore, they slow down. Their bottoms drag along the ocean floor.

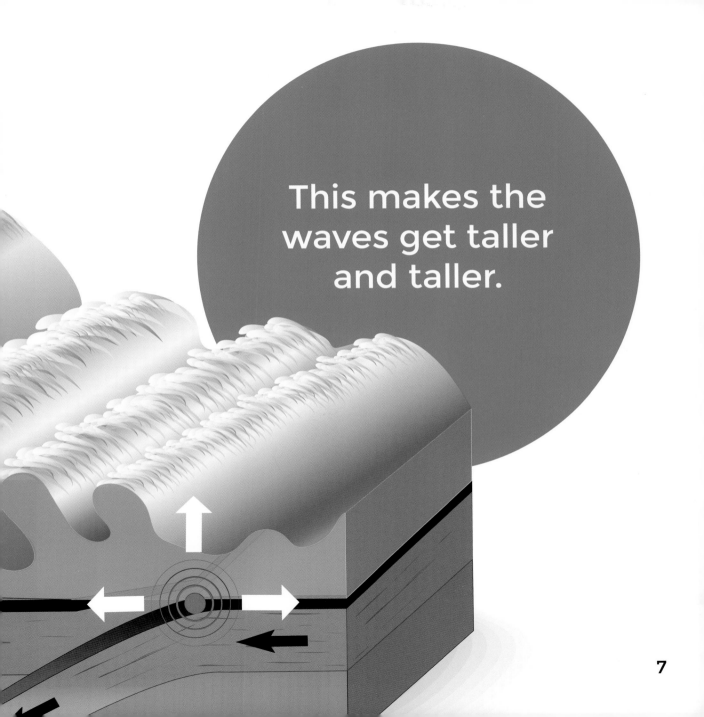

This makes the waves get taller and taller.

Technology

Scientists try to **predict** tsunamis. They look for underwater earthquakes.

They also measure
wave heights and speeds.

Computers use this **data** to make maps. The maps show where a tsunami might hit. Scientists can warn the people in its path.

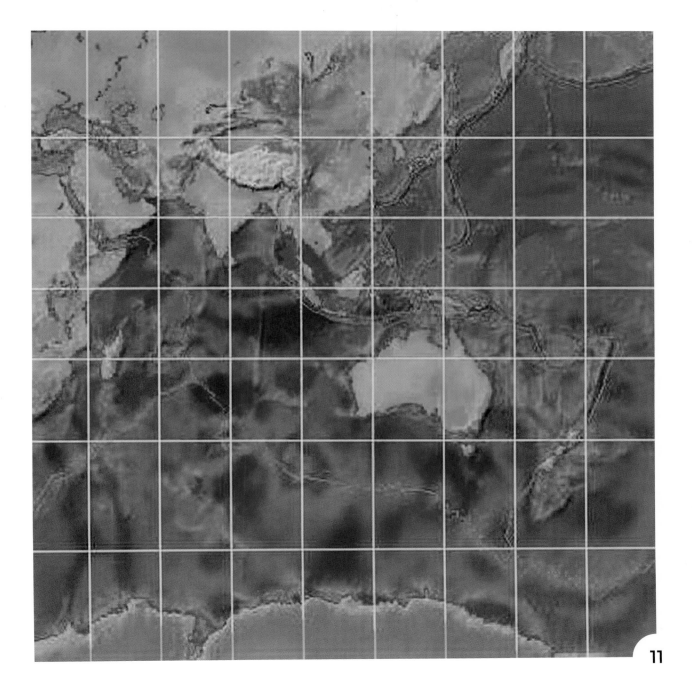

11

Engineering

Tsunami waves can wash away whole cities. Some cities along **coasts** build walls.

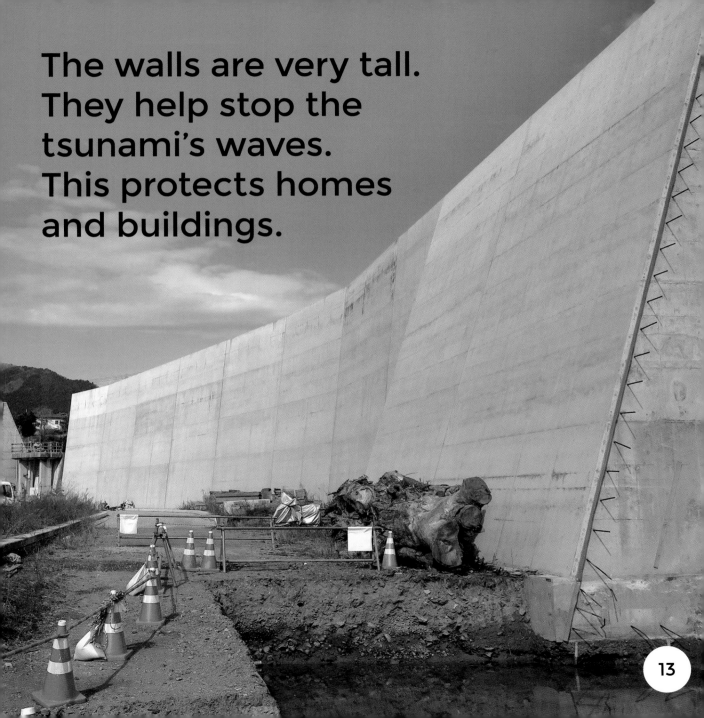

The walls are very tall.
They help stop the
tsunami's waves.
This protects homes
and buildings.

Art

A tsunami hit Thailand in 2004.
Women there made **batik**.

They painted on fabric.
Then they sold it. They used the
money to help rebuild.

Math

Tsunamis start out at sea. But they can hit land that is far away. Some travel thousands of miles from their source.

One tsunami hit California. Its source was more than 6,000 miles (9,656 km) away.

Tsunami waves move fast. Some go 500 miles per hour (805 kmh).

That means waves could go 6,000 miles (9,656 km) in 12 hours!

Key Stats

- More than 70 percent of tsunamis happen in the Pacific Ocean.

- Japan is hit by more tsunamis than any other country.

- Most tsunami waves are less than 10 feet (3 m) tall.

- The highest tsunami wave ever was in Alaska. It was more than 1,720 feet (524 m) tall.

Glossary

batik – fabric with patterns made by putting wax on part of the cloth so it is not colored by dye.

coast – where land and water meet.

data – information that is collected to study or plan something.

earthquake – when part of the earth's surface shakes or trembles.

predict – to guess what might happen in the future.

source – the cause or starting point of something.

Booklinks

For more information on tsunamis, please visit abdobooklinks.com

 In on STEAM!

Learn even more with the Abdo Zoom STEAM database. Check out abdozoom.com for more information.

Index